BASICS OF HILL ENGINEERING

ASHISH SINGH

ISBN 979-888606066-9

This book is basically written on the basis of practical experiences and the problems that we have faced in connecting an isolated village on the top of a hilly feature having an approximate distance of five kilometres from the main connectivity of the market. I would like to thank **Mr. Aditya Gaur,** who is the actual mastermind behind this track and I would also like to thank my co-author **Mr. Rafik Ahmed,** a highly experienced man when it comes to connecting rural areas to the mainland, in this project who helped me in anticipating various problems beforehand only and together we found the solutions for various problems that we encountered. This work is totally based on our practical field experiences. This book **doesn't deal with civil-engineering aspects or any other engineering solutions.** This book is basically for the raw beginners who doesn't like too much of theory and formulae of engineering branches and rather are **interested in solving the problems on ground with the availability of limited resources.** It only consists of method of providing a better communication and connectivity to isolated hilly areas, where the reach of vehicles is not possible.

Contents

Acknowledgements

Mr Rafik Ahmed, The Co-Author

"Chalo kuch naye raaste banaayen, Jin par chalkar hum ek dusre se jud saken aur vikaas kaarya ko badhava mil sake."

"Let's construct new roads, over which we can walk and connect to each other and develop the nation."

Prologue

In the subsequent chapters we are going to discuss and talk about connecting Rural hilly areas to the prominent markets. In this, we are going to discuss regarding the creation of a track in hilly areas by simpler and economical means on the basis of personal practical experiences on ground. I won't be discussing any rocket-science technology which will be difficult for my non-engineer readers to understand. Layman language is used for the better understanding of readers.

CHAPTER ONE

Hill Cutting & Common Problems

As we started our journey to this isolated hilly region of Arunachal Pradesh, India, we saw a village having almost five hundred metres of vertical height from the base (from the main market region). We, me and two of my other subordinates, decided to climb the top. When we reached the peak of it, we happened to witness a beautiful hamlet with yaks wandering and grazing here and there around it. Now, rather going deep into the beauty of that village, or how and from where we managed resources, I will directly come to the problems and the solutions that we anticipated for the people living there. Having a good and deep interaction with the villagers living, we realised that the village though a part of our territory is devoid of the riches of our mainland. We figured out three main and basic necessities that the villagers living on the top were in the dire need of.

There was **no road connectivity, no light and no water storage facility nearby, though there used to rain heavily.** These were the three major problems that we were supposed to solve.

HOW TO IMPROVE RURAL COMMUNICATION IN HILLS?

Yes exactly!!! This was the question that stroke our grey.

We all know that connecting rural villages of hilly areas is one of the biggest problems that our government is facing and is working hard to achieve it. We too tried our hands out on this problem in our own manner and it really taught us a lot about dealing problems on ground.

To do this, we selected the shortest approach towards the village from the base of the main market. Though, we were successful in finding the shortest approach, but this was the approach which used to **flood with rainwater**. We started our working on sunny days, completely unaware of this menace. Steps we followed –

1. **Finding out the shortest possible distance** from the bottom to the top. We named our bottom most point, from where we started working as **SP** (starting point) and top most point as **FP** (final point).

a. **How to go by this?**

To get our hands on this, we were required to find the Vertical Interval. What is this Vertical Interval?

To understand this, we have to first find out the Vertical heights of both SP and FP from main sea level.

So, the vertical interval or VI in short is,

$VI = V_2 - V_1;$

where V_2 and V_1 are vertical heights of FP and SP from mean-sea level.

Thus, to find the desirable distance with a desirable gradient we needed to find the Horizontal Equivalent. Horizontal equivalent is basically the ratio of VI to the slope which we want in mountains (I have taken it to be 1:10).

In this case, my VI was 500 metres. So, my horizontal equivalent became 5000 metres, which was the distance along with suitable gradient of the top-most point from the bottom most point, simply between FP and SP.

b. **Why suitable gradient?**

Suitable gradient so as to let the personal and commercial carriers to connect the village to the main market.

c. The most important step is the **integration of the above two steps and finding out the total number of turning points.** It is more important to decide the location and the distance between each turning point (TP). The distance between each **TP** should be in-sync with the average distributed distance of all TPs and the gradient factor.

2. **Excavation and amount of excavation** is the second basic task which falls in when we are planning to connect such a location as discussed above to the main populated area.

a. How to go by it?

It's actually not a cake walk to do the excavation part. We were lucky to manage an excavating machine operator (we used JS201 model of JCB), a 20-tonne excavating machine.

3. There were numerous **problems that we encountered during reconnaissance** of the hill for the track and were as under—

a. **Electric lines**

These were the old electric lines that were laid years ago but due to the lightning and heavy rains many trees fell down on these lines creating electricity problems for the village and a major obstacle in front of us. These lines were 10-12 ft high from the ground which actually is a major obstacle for the mobility of hill cutting plants (JS201 i.e., 20 tonne excavator).

Solution: Diverted the track direction, as much as possible from the, away from the electric lines that were prone to fall at any time.

b. **Excessive uncontrolled drainage of water** over the track from the above of hills

There is no particular direction for the flow of this excessive water down the hill. So, again there was a challenge in front of us to select a track which allowed a minimum seepage of water. The need for this was to save the material from getting drained along with water which we will be requiring for the construction of track.

Solution: Again, we followed the same mantra of diverting the track away from the heavy flow of water but too much diverting was not possible as we had to see the above discussed menace too. So, we directed the flow either in between two turning points or at the **ends of turning points.** Why in between?

In between so as to construct a culvert between the tracks to channelise the excess flow of water and regarding ends of turning points I will discuss later.

c. **Hard rock**

While exploring the path for the track cutting we encountered several hard-rock patches. So, we marked many of them for drilling and later blasting, but were really huge and were way beyond our capacity to blast.

Solution: The solution was to make turning points at huge rock sites.

d. Hard Slope

It is very important to modify a hard slope into an easier one comparatively as it will provide an ease to the commuters moving up and down the hill on a daily basis. We need to understand that public vehicles can only go up to the slope of 1:10 and it really becomes difficult for them if the slope increases.

Solution: In such a situation, we have to increase the numbers of turning points. This will solve the problem of gradient of the track, though there will be a sufficient increase in the distance to the destination.

e. Sliding Zone

During reconnaissance we identified various sliding zones. These can be easily identified as a fresh chunk of land as compared to the surrounding area of land.

Solution: In such a place, we need to construct retaining wall and breast walls (these terms are explained in the subsequent chapters).

f. Soft Soil

Due to the excessive water flow from above the hill, there were many areas where we encountered soft soil. Now, What exactly is soft soil? It is basically patch of land which becomes slushy or marshy due to the over deposition of unwanted water and is the reason for the formation of puddles on the path. This reduces the soil strength and the soil continuously flows down the hill resulting in landslides.

Solution: Such a patch should be avoided for any constructions.

g. Blind Turns

Blind turns again are one of the major problems while doing a reconnaissance for the track construction. Major because its not easy to identify a turn which can turn into a blind turn. A blind turn is one where there is a high possibility of accidents due to the presence of sharp turnings and less time for the driver to react.

Solution: Only possible solution for this problem is increasing the turning radius at the turning points (TPs).

h. Sliding of a turning point

While making turning points with the help of an excavating machine or earth moving plants, the turning points become weak and due to the reduced strength of turning point it starts sliding and slides over the turning point just below it. Due to this, there is always a fear of loosing the excavating machine and the operator.

Solution: While working under such clandestine conditions, a crane along with the **steel wire rope held to the back of excavating machine** is of utmost requirement. The machine will keep excavating along with steel wire rope held to its back and to the crane.

i. Heavy Rainfall

Heavy rainfall is one of the biggest challenges in the hills of Arunachal Pradesh, India. So, while working for the hill cutting it is imperative to know which all intervals we can get to work.

Solution: We cannot be one hundred percent certain regarding the rainfall. It can happen at any time. So, we should be prepared with raincoat, waterproof jackets, umbrellas, **waterproof explosives and waterproof cement.**

j. Snowfall

Snowfall is yet again one of the biggest challenges to work in North-east India especially the higher hills of Arunachal Pradesh. Thus, biting cold and chilling winters makes it next to impossible for the people to work openly on the hill.

Solution: From mid-November till mid-March, the track work should be halted.

k. Safety Challenges

While, excavation machine being employed on the construction of higher turning points, there is always a fear of big boulders or sharp pointed rocks to fall over the workers preparing lower turning points. This may sometimes causes fatal casualties and injuries to the people working on lower regions of the same hill.

Solution: Every person working on the track should wear designated **helmets**. There should be person along with excavating machine to pass the message to the person working on the lower region with the help of a **walkie-talkie**.

l. **Lack of communication**

Due to the lack of sufficient mobile towers in the hilly areas, there is always a communication gap.

Solution: Adequate walkie-talkies, whistles and body signals to be employed while working. The whole of the route from starting point to the last turning point should be numbered on turning point basis.

m. **Failing of survey equipment due to bad weather conditions**

Due to bad weather conditions in hilly areas, the whole of the area becomes extremely foggy and this causes malfunctioning of both survey equipment and GPS.

Solution: Manual compass, Abney level and hand-made measuring tapes can be subsequently employed.

After successfully completing our task i.e., cutting the hill from the bottom till top for the track construction till the beginning of the November month, we left the track virgin for next six months. WHY?

Deeply pondering over all the previous experiences, we came to know that if we immediately initiate working over the freshly-cut track, it would become a very arduous task for us to identify the sliding zones on the track, in addition, winters too were arriving over the horizon. What is the need to identify the sliding zones?

Cutting a hill for track construction though is a very important task, but it is more important to sustain that track for years. For it to sustain over a long duration of time, permanent works plays a prominent role and you can't simply site permanent works according to your will. Siting of permanent works should always be according to nature's will. So, ideally a freshly cut track without permanent works over it should be left over for an year, but due to time-shortage we can left it for a minimum duration of six-months, since, in the next six months the track will witness a variations of climate and weather and their extreme effects over it. **It is in this duration only that the track will be full of landslides at various places on it. Plus, the heavy rains will form a natural drainage system for the water to flow down up from the hill.** And this is exactly what we are in need of to initiate the most needed permanent works over the track. It will assist us in identifying the total number of retaining and breast walls needed for the track and the natural drainage line of rainwater will help us in identifying the amount of length we are in need of for drainage line construction.

Identifying the correct number of walls and the drainage length is helpful in minimum wastage of resources and human effort. Plus, it also makes the project an economical one.

CHAPTER TWO

Permanent Works

Introduction

As the name suggests, this chapter will be dealing with the kind of permanent works that are needed in the hilly areas where there is seepage of water and the hills which are having comparatively lower seepage. One thing is for sure that seepage will be there in the hills of north-east India, and one can't deny this fact. It is due to the seepage of water from the hill that our track, which we were constructing used to become slushy and made it next to impossible for even 4x4 four-wheelers to reach the destination, which for them was the village on top. Identifying this problem at the earliest gave us enough time to think of possible permanent works which can be employed to reduce the adversity of track on the locals.

And many a times, it too happened that a chunk of loosely held soil too slide over the track, basically a landslide. So, this also hampered our work by delaying our daily labour hours. Once, it happened that whole of the upper track fell down over immediate down track and it too was a kind of landslide. Now, we had two major challenges. First one was to avoid landslides over the tracks and secondly to save the freshly cut track from sliding down.

The possible solution for this menace, where plenty of seepage used to take place was the construction of **gravity type** permanent works. Under gravity type permanent works we have retaining walls and breast walls.

1. Gravity Type Permanent Works
Construction of Retaining Walls & Breast Walls

a. Retaining Wall

What is a retaining wall?

As the time flows, the constructed track reduces its strength and there are probable chances of it sliding downwards few centimetres every second. To avoid this kind of situation, a construction of a mixture of stones, cement and sand is very much required. This construction we term it as a retaining wall. The standard dimensions that we have followed were **8m x 3m x 1.8m** (length x height x thickness). The passive advantages of retaining walls are:

(i). Increase in the road width and turning radius at turning points.

(ii).Re-claiming of the lost piece of land while excavating.

Note:- It is highly recommended to construct retaining walls at turning points. Since at turning points the speed of the vehicles is low and it spends more time as compared to the rest of the track. So, a high stability and strength is required at turning points.

Point to keep in mind while excavating the base of the retaining wall is to place sentries at the TPs and track beneath the excavation site at a safety place with proper safety gears. In addition to it, all of the sentries should have communication device with them or if it costs too much then a whistle can do the same. Always prefer to excavate with the help of heavy excavator. Since rooting out soil from the site requires a great amount of machine power.

A Retaining Wall

b. Breast Wall

What is a breast wall?

A construction which basically avoids the debris to fall over the freshly cut piece of land/track in the hilly areas is termed as a breast wall. It is always constructed on the upper side as we walk to the top from the bottom of the hill.

Why?

A breast wall brings stability to the freshly cut track by holding the soil in-position at a very fast rate. The dimensions are same as of retaining wall 8mx3mx1.8m.

Prefer using a medium excavator (for rocky strata) or a light excavator to excavate for breast wall base. Reason being, a heavy excavator may disturb the upper region of the breast wall site and may lead to a landslide over the selected breast wall site.

A Breast Wall

Planning and excavation of retaining wall and breast wall.

(i). Whenever the siting of both the walls are near to each other then, according to my experience of working in hills, I advise first to excavate retaining wall and later breast wall, as the soil from breast wall while excavating can be directly utilised in the upper region of retaining wall so as to level (uniformly) it with the main track.

(ii). Whenever two or more than two breast walls are sited along with each other, then no gap between the walls is advisable. Since, two or more than two walls are selected at critical sites of landslides, so, a gap between the walls will act as a leakage point for the land/loosely held soil to erode down to the track, causing a blockage of the track. In addition, it will weaken the combined strength of the walls. In case, if a gap is leftover between the two walls, that gap can be occupied with the erection of hesco bags one over the other.

(iii). Time-period between wall excavation and construction over it should not exceed two days. Since freshly excavated, there are probable chances of sliding of track land over it.

(iv). The raw material for the next day task should be filled in the tippers and dumpers in the same evening as it will save the time which the vehicle and the machine will take to start (due to cold climate it takes around an hour for the tippers and dumpers to start in the morning). Always fill the tippers with the help of a mini excavator and utilise heavy excavators for a extreme jobs.

Note:- Retaining walls are responsible for the existence of track (because if the retaining walls are weak then the track upon it is compromised) whereas breast walls are responsible for avoiding landslides over the track. Breast walls reduces the width of the track whereas retaining walls enhances the width of the track.

What all we need to construct a retaining wall/ breast wall?

Whenever we are constructing a retaining wall, the first and the foremost thing is the base excavation of the wall. This can be done by any excavating machine depending on the time factor we are considering. This is the time when we have to be careful regarding the dimensions of the wall. Accuracy we can't achieve by just excavating it with the machine but an endeavour to achieve maximum of it should be made. During excavation, make sure that an excavation depth of minimum 500mm is made by the operator. This is important for a stable wall structure. Once the base is prepared, the next step is soling of that base. Soling is done by filling big boulders of palm size and later 63-90mm rocks in the voids. The leftover voids are filled with 40mm boulders.

After the soling is done, the next step is PCC over the soled base. This PCC is in the ratio of 1:4:8. For a layman, it simply means one bag of cement, four bags of sand and 8 bags of aggregate (bajri). A mixture of all three is prepared in the listed ratio and is levelled over the soled base of the wall. The unfinished wall is then left over for two days for the PCC base to solidify completely. One thing to keep in mind, never left the PCC base to remain uncovered. Before leaving the site after finishing a day's work always cover the fresh PCC with a plastic covering. This is done in order to save it from the unpredicted weather conditions like rainfall.

After leaving the wall for two days, immediately work should be started over the PCC base. The next step is the use of natural rocks of the desired dimension to erect the wall. I won't be discussing the pattern of how to lay rocks one over the other as the mason is better at this job. Wall should be nine to ten ft high to achieve the desired dimensions. Again, when the wall has achieved the desired dimensions, the top of it needs a PCC topping for achieving a stable structure. Minimum thickness of it should be 15cms. The backfilling of the walls is done with the help of soil and rocks. The excavated land should be refilled into the walls and should be properly rammed with the help of a rammer.

Weepholes

These are basically the outlets that are left within the retaining and breast walls. Generally, PVC pipes of around 0.75 metres are placed in these holes for the easy exit of the overflowing water on the tracks. Their main function is to save the erosion of walls from excessive rainwater or track water from the top of the hills. The quantity of weepholes in a wall depends totally on the climate of the region where construction takes place.

2. The **third major challenge** that we faced was **extreme rainfall**. Though, heavy rainfall itself created a drainage system for it over the track, but most of it was useless and was affecting the track by eroding away the soil of the track with it. Thus, the patches experiencing such a condition are leftover with a rocky-strata which further leads to reduction in the tire-track traction of the vehicle. So, we were in need of a proper drainage line that could cater for the unnecessary flow of water down the track and could avoid the erosion of soil down the track. To counter this menace, we identified the construction of culverts and drainage line along the track.

a. Culvert

It is basically a passage for the water to pass through the freshly cut track. It is done in order to avoid the flow of water on track which may lead to the erosion of the soil from the track. It is really important as it is needed for the credible stability of the track. Its dimensions are dependent on the flow of water through the track. Half width of the culvert is made first and the remaining half is made once the first half is completed. It is done in this fashion, just to regulate the track traffic efficiently. Once the culvert is made, the side walls at the bottom, just besides the hume pipes are made in the shape of funnel, so as to direct the overflowing water through the pipes. It is very important to regularly check the culverts, if they are constructed near to a sliding zone. Since culverts are more prone to get clogged from the landslide and the water may come over the track in such a case. In addition, it is also important to inspect the hume pipes are free from any kind of big boulders or rocks inside them, as during the rainfall when the soil erodes with water, it gets stuck to the obstruction inside the pipes, which further may lead to the deposition of more and more soil, thereby blocking the whole of culvert and the water may take its way over the track and leads to erosion of soil to the bottom of the track.

Culvert with Eight hume pipes

Obstructions should be checked for, once the construction is finished especially in the case of culverts and drainage line. The wing walls acts as a funnel for the water coming down from the top of the hill. The down hill side can be excused from the wing-wall construction so as to increase the economy of the project. A perfect construction is of utmost importance on the up hill side so as to avoid the water ruining track by weeping through different ways to bottom.

b. **Drainage line**

You cannot construct culvert everywhere thus it may again lead to the erosion of the soil down from the freshly cut track. So, in order to avoid this, we generally construct drain lines. Now, as the name suggests—it is a drainage line passage for the water to go down the hill via a proper drainage system which is constructed along the track towards the inner side i.e., towards the uphill side. These are again of many types depending on the terrain. Measurements that we selected were 45cm (base PCC), 15cm thick and 30cm height (side wall of drainage line) and 1:15 (slope). The importance of side wall is that it avoids the seepage of water beneath the base and it only happens when adequate depth has been provided for the wall to support the base. The slope angle is not fixed, it may so happen that at overflowing water sites, more of gradient is required for that section of the drainage line.

A line drain

Construction of a drainage line

All permanent constructions on hills follow a similar pattern and so is drainage line. The very first step is earth work i.e., excavation for the drainage line with the help of a suitable excavating machine and following the desired dimensions of the drainage system which is to be constructed.

(i). **Soling** of the drainage line is the very first step that is generally followed. Soling is done with the help of 40 mm rocks and then a layering of comparatively smaller size rocks takes place. Soling is done so as to hold the mixture of sand, cement and aggregate together.

Mistake and Lesson learnt

Just to save few days I tried a stunt actually a blunder, which costed me weeks. The mistake that I done was that I told my men to skip the soling part and directly spread the mixture (sand, cement and aggregate) over the freshly cut drainage line. Everything seemed perfect till the time we left the site. At night it rained heavily and all the mixture drained to the down slope and got deposited at the end of the twenty metres drainage line. So, the lesson that I learnt from this mishap was to never skip the soling part as it forms the strong base for a completely finished drainage line. It grips the mixture and reduces the draining of sand, cement and aggregate mixture.

(ii). After the soling is done, the next step is to spread the mixture over the drainage line and cast the mixture into the desired dimensions. This step is called as **PCC base** step of drainage line.

(iii). The third and final step is erection of the **side wall line** of drainage line which is along with the base PCC. The dimensions are as per need and as per terrain requirements. The walls are casted with the help of ply wood sheets. These ply wood sheets are erected and are held to each other in pairs and in between them, the mixture is filled. The mixture is same (sand, cement and aggregate).

Note:- Second and third steps can be inter-changed as per individual choice.

Planning of work on drainage line

While working on a drainage line, you cannot simultaneously work on both, the side wall and the base of the drainage line, so planning should be in such a manner that either side wall work should be leading or base work should be ahead. For this, I suggest dividing the team into three parties (party strength as per need). Side wall party, base work party and soling party. Soling party can be utilised for other minor works related to drainage line too.

Reason why side wall work and base work can't be done simultaneously is that if we do them together then, once the mixture and wall line get solidified and the moment we will remove the thin ply wood sheets from the side walls, a gap line will be formed between the base and the side wall.

It is recommended to first erect the side walls of the drainage line and then do the bottom PCC for the base over the soled drainage line. It is highly recommended to fill the vacant space behind the wall with rocks and fill the remaining voids with the soil from surroundings and tamp it nicely. This makes the side wall structure highly stable and prevents further wrecking of it from the falling rocks from the hills. In addition, this also prevents the water from the hills top to fall behind the wall structure, thereby preventing the seepage of water into the track. Moreover, it is very common that the rocks from the top fall over the drainage line there by obstructing the muddy water. Due, to this obstruction the soil well mixed with the flowing water deposits over the rock blockage and gets solidified with time and thereby diverting the rainwater off the drainage line to the track. This makes the track slushy and a big problem for the mobility of vehicles.

Modification in drainage line

Modifications in drainage line can save human effort, raw material and most importantly time. How? While working on the track in the month of October when there is a gap between rainy season and snowfall in the north-east, we discovered that the chunk of water flowing through the track, where earlier there was a need of a culvert, has dried-up. Seeing this as an opportunity, we avoid constructing culvert over that site, instead we made a modified drainage line with both the peripheries (width-wise) having a drainage wall, which will basically prevent the over flow of excessive rainwater during the rainy season. By doing this we not only saved the extra cement, sand and aggregate but also we saved Hume pipes which will be needed to construct a culvert.

Sequence of action

There is no sacrosanct sequence of action for such projects. These all are time, terrain and weather dependent. However, there is a general and logical approach that we followed for our project. Sequence of action that one must follow in general while constructing a track should be –

Firstly, eighty percent of the **culverts** must be completed.

Once the culverts are done, the **undrained line** passage should be immediately erected so as to channelise the over flowing water on the track. Once, this water menace is under control only then the

walls erection should come into focus, otherwise it really becomes difficult to work under slushy soil conditions of the freshly cut track. Why unlined drain first? Reason being—if lined drains are constructed then afterwards of it, the construction of walls, especially breast walls will distort the newly constructed drainage line. So, it is highly preferred to construct unlined drains.

After the channelising of water is done rightly, breast walls and retaining walls should be of subsequent priority. This is done, so as to stabilise the track from the soil erosion and landslides. It is the slow and steady soil erosion which gives birth to big landslides. So, this factor should never be despised.

Track Improvement Means

a. When the gradient is high

Solution: Rigid Pavement

A construction which is made on soft patches or at critical points to enhance the stability of the track. It is basically made from the same 1:4:8 ratio of cement, sand and aggregate. Though it is not a very difficult task to cover the critical patch with it, but again as I said before, everything is situation and circumstances based. The **major challenge** that we faced while curing the soft patches with rigid pavement was:

(i). The track was the only track connecting the hamlet on the top to the main market. So, it was not viable for us to completely spread the ratio in a one go, as it will halt the basic need supply vehicles' movement from the main market to the village.

Solution: We decided to do it in parts i.e., two metres of rigid pavement first and once it dries up then the other half will be catered for the same. Though it was a wonderful solution but the failure occurred when most of the vehicles were passing over the freshly done PCC part. And thus, all our efforts went in vain. The solution to this problem was dividing the width of the track into three parts and doing it part by part. We divided 4 metres width of the road into three equal parts of 1.33 metres.

Sequence that we followed for completing the rigid pavement was:

We completed the left side first, right side afterwards and then the mid portion of the track. The reason we followed this pattern was that firstly doing left side allowed the movement of the vehicles from the unconstructed mid and right-side portion. Once the left side was solidified, the right side was done. While the right side was fresh, the vehicles passed from left-side and the mid portion and subsequently the mid portion too was made. While I was on the right-side of the rigid pavement, an idea stroke my mind and that was to leave the mid-portion to maintain economy of the rigid pavement idea. So, out of total three rigid pavements, I followed this idea for the very first rigid pavement but the result was disastrous. Due to the continuous flow of water from the mid, all the material from the left and the right side got washed away and hence it costed us wasted of time, effort and manpower.

Based on this experience we completed the remaining two rigid pavements successfully.

b. When the gradient is normal

Solution: When the gradient is normal and the track is either too slushy or too rocky, then the patching of that portion is done by the layering of 63-90mm first and subsequently the smaller rock sizes. The layering is totally dependent on the ground need and there is no fixed quantity rule to spread the stones over the worse patches. Further, the spreading can be done by any of the three methods (complete, 3-parts or turtle method), based on the need of the hour. Spreading is totally based on the fact of filling as much voids as viable, to make the track layers more compact and stable.

5. Hesco bag wall

It is basically a substitute to breast walls. Hesco bag walls are employed at places where there is risk of soil erosion or land sliding at a dry patch area. Avoid the Hesco bag wall erection at wet sliding zones as the soil may come out of the pores of the bag, making the bag bulge outwards and reducing its track life. The walls dimensions are independent of a general worldwide standard and is totally dependent on the need and employment of the bags at the selected sites. It serves exactly the same purpose i.e., keeps the sliding land intact.

A hesco bag wall

6. Passing Places

As the name suggests, passing places serves the purpose for the vehicles to pass each other in hilly areas. They are ideally at a distance of 500 metres away from each other, but there can be slight variations as it is terrain dependent variable and can vary according to the need and terrain. The standard dimensions that we selected— length= 7.5m and width= 3m. Preferably passing places should be made rigid i.e., PCC basing is preferred to make the place stable for the vehicles to rest over it in hilly terrain. In addition to the above, retaining walls too are highly recommended when the passing places are unsupported by the hill side.

A Passing Place

7. Soling

After completing the permanent works, complete focus should be given on strengthening the track. Strengthening of the track is done by the means of soling the track. Soling is basically the process of making layers over the track. Now, why soling is needed? I know that this is the least probable question that have strike your grey. Soling is basically done for two major purposes— Saving the track soil from getting washed away to the bottom due to the heavy overflow of rainwater. Secondly, it provides a grip and a uniform layer for the vehicles to commute from top to bottom and vice-versa.

First layer soling (Initial soling with 63-90mm rocks)

It Involves:

a. **Levelling**: It is generally done with the help of a mini dozer. While working on hills banking of the track is preferred unlike in plains where cambering is done to the path. In banking of the track the outer slope to the hill is raised at a small gradient. So the operator working on the dozer should be seriously advised to keep the gradient factor in his mind. Once the levelling is done, compactor is rolled twice over the levelled surface to settle down the track soil for subsequent action.

b. **Spreading of 63-90mm rocks on the levelled surface**: On obtaining a well levelled surface, the next very important step is spreading of 63-90mm rocks over the surface of the track. Spreading is generally preferred with any of the desired plants. Spreading of rocks will be discussed subsequently. Once the spreading of these rocks is done, compactor is rolled over the rocky surface five to six times.

c. **Spreading of 40mm rocks over 63-90mm rocks**: Once the compaction of the 63-90mm rock layer is done, the next step is spreading of 40mm rocks over the previous layer. This is done in order to fill the voids of the previously spread rock layer. Once again, when the spreading is done, the compactor is rolled over it four to five times.

d. **Spreading of 20mm rocks**: After the compaction of the previous layer, the new layer of 20mm rocks is spread over it. Again, this is done in order to fill the voids of the previous layer. After layering with 20mm rocks, the surface is again rolled by the compactor four to five times. This is the final layering of the track in hills. After the compaction, water is spread over the tracks and is left for a day. On the very next day, the compactor is again rolled over it. This time eight to ten rolls of compactor are necessary for increasing the stability of the track. This is known as pre-final compaction of the track.

e. **Spreading of bajri**: After the compaction of all the previously spread layers, the final step (in our case) was spreading of bajri. Same pattern of spreading is followed as is followed in the above steps.

Methods of Soling the track

a. **Complete method**: This method is preferred when the track traffic is extremely low, limited time frame and extensive manpower and EM(Earth Moving Plants) support.

b. **3-parts method**: This method is highly preferred while working on hilly terrains. In this method the width of the track is divided into three parts and a sequence of spreading is followed. Left side first, then right side and finally the mid-portion of the track is soled. Highly preferred when the track is extremely busy and manpower is limited.

c. **Turtle method**: This method is followed when we have very limited manpower and soling is of secondary focus. Highly recommended to follow this method from the initial phase of the project. As once the project of permanent works is about to get complete, it is also on the verge of completion.

Note:- Since soling is a never-ending process, so in my opinion it should be done passively i.e., should be done along with permanent works. For soling, a dedicated operator of excavator (to spread the soling rocks over the track) and a compactor are sufficient. Furthermore, the dumping of rocks for soling purpose should be dump after the work from the same tippers that were earlier used for dumping raw materials at the sites of permanent works. This way we can avoid wastage of time and the next day operator and compactor can collectively work over the soling site.

Dumping of raw materials

The dumping of raw materials is a very important task and is one of the prominent steps in saving the time and human effort. Hence, dumping should be at least one day prior. The trend that we followed for dumping was once the day's work was over, at the night time we used to park the tippers filled with raw materials on the starting point. This way we could save half an hour that could be consumed to spark the ignition to the tipper engine and to the excavation machine early in the morning. So, saving half an hour of the next day added to the welfare of the project workers.

CHAPTER THREE

Planning

Planning plays an important role when we are undertaking such a big project. It is imperative to plan beforehand only for the smooth functioning of all working parties. It is not only the labour needs that we have to cater for the construction of track in such areas, but administrative side too should be well taken care of. A well-planned project saves a lot of money and time and yes it also provides a perfect welfare to the working class of the project. To have a better planning it is very important to distribute individual responsibilities to various units/teams working under the project. Other than assigning individual duties to the teams, coordination amongst those teams is of utmost importance to execute paper plan on the ground.

The most important task under planning is the selection of route for trace cutting. Generally, to select the route for trace cut an initial recce is performed by the recce team. But in areas where snowfall becomes a menace for the commuters, it is very important to select the right route for the construction of track. The initial blunder that we did was we only recced the route once and that too in clear weather conditions, which undoubtedly gave us a route for the trace cutting. The problem was that this route was covered between two hilly features and was devoid/ late sunlight in winters over the track.

Devoid of sunlight over the track especially during winters was a big disadvantage for the team to complete the task on time and also it was very risky for the local people there to use vehicles over the track, even with the tyre chains. The accumulation of snow over the track and continuous initial movement of the vehicles over it compressed the snow and turned it into a hard glassy surface, thereby reducing friction and causing the vehicles to slip over it.

The only possible permanent relief to this menace was to initially site the trace cutting correctly. By siting it correctly I mean- to select the feature which gets the maximum sunlight of the day. As it will melt the snow to a maximum limit, thereby catalysing the working speed of various parties and reducing the life-risk for commuters/locals, using the track for daily basis.

The various parties that are needed for the construction of track are:

a. Working parties

(i). Culvert party

(ii). Drainage Line party

(iii). Breast Wall party

(iv). Retaining Wall party

(v). Soling and Compaction party

(vi). Snow Clearing party (provides the snow clearance and green signal to both- the working parties and the local commuters.)

b. Administration party

(i). Site planning party: Main executing body of the whole project. Comprised of senior engineers, experienced on ground junior engineers, a draftsman.

Siting and employment of various working parties is the sole task of this body. A part from siting, it also takes care of ultimatum of the higher authorities

i.e., the time factor.

(ii). Belly-timber party (feeding party): It comprises of cooks, dedicated team of breakfast and lunch distributors to the labourers working on the different

sites of hill.

(iii). Project-stores party: This party is responsible for providing all kinds of gears and instruments that are needed by the working parties. Items to be issued

Individually to everyone.

c. MT party (Mechanical Transport): It includes a vehicle mechanic over two vehicles, electrician for general circuits inside vehicles, Vehicle Sensor Specialist for vehicles. Distribution of Vehicles is as follows:

(i). Belly-timber party vehicle.

(ii). A light vehicle for site planning party.

(iii). Dedicated vehicles for labour party (to drop them on the work site and bring them back after the day's work).

(iv). A contingency vehicle for the vehicle and earth moving plant's mechanic.

(v). Tippers and dumpers to dump the raw material at the working sites.

(vi). Sand-cement-aggregate mixture machines as per individual project need.

(vii). Fuel, oil and lubrication (FOL) party.

Note:- Reason to use separate vehicle for separate parties is to ensure the minimum waste of time and efficient execution of the project plan as planned by the site-planning party.

d. EM plant party (Earth Moving): It includes an EM plant mechanic over two plants, Sensor specialist. It is very important to have a specialist when we are dealing with heavy earth moving plants. Since, many a times it may happen that the plant be off-track in the middle of the track. So, that is the time when a highly trained mechanic can save the time by doing the needful. Plants under this party are as follows:

1. A heavy excavator: Used to excavate and prepare base for retaining walls. Sometimes, used to clear major landslides too that frequently occurs on the

track during heavy rains.

2. A dozer: Used to level the unlevelled track. Generally useful during the initial alignment of the track.

3. Compactor: Used at the end for compaction of the rocks that are spread over the track during soling of the track.

4. A light excavator (Tata Hitachi 7 tonne approximately): This is generally used to fill the raw materials in the tippers.

5. A medium excavator: Used to excavate the base for breast walls or to clear the minor landslides over the track during rainy seasons.

Note:- While working on hills, it is better to use more of the wheeled earth moving plants than tracked plants. Reason being, the wheeled plants provide a great mobility and chances of its failure are extremely less than those of tracked plants. In case of tracked plants, the heavy metallic chain over which the metallic wheels rotate has a high chance of failure which restricts the mobility of the plant. In addition, the metallic chain, while the plant movement roots out the soil from the track.

Movement of mixture machines

1. Down-slope movement: While shifting the mixture machine down the slope from one working site to the other, after completing the previous site's work, it is very important that it should be loaded either inside a tipper or a dumper with the help of a medium or heavy excavator and should never be done manually. The reason being, it is a wheeled thing and as we take it down the slope, it gradually increases its speed and it becomes impossible for the machine to stop by the working party. It will lead to injury to the labourers working and may also fall from the cliff to the bottom, thereby losing an important resource. Hence, it should be loaded inside a tipper/dumper and should be properly anchored inside it. To load the machine, tie the critical ends of the machine to the steel wire rope and pick the machine up with the help of a heavy or medium excavator and firmly stabilise it inside the tipper/dumper.

2.Up-slope movement: The upslope movement of the mixture machine is comparatively easy and can be taken manually to the fresh working site if the distance is 100 metres or less with a suitable gradient. Otherwise, always take it to the next location with the help of earth-moving plants. Two guides should be present to guide the driver at the turning points. One at the front and other at the rear (instructing the front guide).

e. Medical Team Party comprising of an ambulance, a doctor and a nurse on stand-by.

Selection of raw material

Sand

Sand is of two types. First one is, the sand that we get from the river beds. And the second kind is what we get from the hills. Now, the question arises, which one out of these is best. Based on my personal experience I prefer the first one i.e., the one from the river beds. This sand is more stable than the one from the hills. It jells up faster and completely with the cement and mixture than the other one. Hence, it provides a longer life to the permanent works. Sand should be free of silt content and other foreign substances. Sieve the sand before use.

Cement

Preferably a higher-grade cement is recommended while working at such terrain. It is very important to keep the cement isolated from moisture and water as it leads to the hardening of the cement and renders it useless. A special insulated storage for the cement should be made to protect it from external factors. The height of the cement stack should not be more than fifteen bags to prevent the possibility of lumping up under pressure. The basic principle to use during the consumption of cement bags is 'First In First Out' (FIFO).

Coarse aggregate

Natural aggregates should be given first priority. The aggregates should be stored on flat surfaces. While storing aggregates on the working site, make sure it dumped away from the track to avoid its wastage. Always store fine and coarse aggregates separately. Wash the coarse aggregates prior usage. Use only graded aggregates for permanent works.

Water

Water should be free from any deleterious material. The pH value of water should not be less than 6 i.e., it should not show acidic characteristics. Generally potable water is considered satisfactory for mixing concrete. Adequate water storage and carrying facility to be made at various working sites on the track.

Admixture

In case if any admixture is used for special concreting, note down the type and purpose of admixture. In our case we used quick setting compound, since the climate is generally rainy or snowy so it becomes difficult for concrete to settle down if admixture is not used.

Selection of working site

Site selection is the most important task which the site-planning team undertakes. Though, it is really very important to identify the sliding zones to construct walls upon them, but at the same employment of various parties as per climate and weather conditions is the priority. The top hill constructions should be initiated at clear weather conditions and the down part hill constructions should be left for worse weather conditions. Reason being, the more closer working parties are to the base, the faster they can start working and close-in fast, when the weather is unpredictable and at the same, some of the output can be achieved from the working parties even at worse weather conditions. The logic here is not to keep the working strength at the base in worse weather conditions, but closer to the administration and accommodation base of the project teams.

In addition to this, the jobs that requires extreme human efforts and machine efforts should be planned during favourable climatic conditions and the minor jobs to be kept for a bad season. This will assist in completing the job right on time/ before time.

Siting the location for various teams

The siting of location of various parties is yet again an important thing. It just requires the ground study of the area where the base is to be made and a logical approach. The siting should be in a manner that location of all the teams is closer to the main administrative base. This is because administration team is the final executing body. So, the closer the other teams are sited to the administration base, the faster and flexible will be the decision making by the administration team. Preferably the administration base should be cited at the central location to all the other bases.

The bases that are needed:

1. Administration base.
2. Accommodation base.
3. Mechanical Transport base.
4. Medical base.
5. Cook house and Mess.
6. Project-stores base.

Failure of EM plants while doing a job

There was a small accident that happened with me, while I was with a light weight excavator on the track. I told the plant operator to excavate for the retaining wall with the help of that plant. Though, I knew that it will be a difficult job for the plant, but seeing the soil mix boulder strata I took the call that the plant will be suitable for excavation. To my shock, after few minutes the operator came running to me and informed me that one hydraulic pipe started leaking and is unable to take the excavation load.

Learning: First of all, at the least, a medium excavator should be employed for such a task and secondly another plant should be at stand-by while the first is working on that site.

Uneven track surface during heavy rainfall

It is a very common situation which occurs during heavy rainfalls. During heavy rains, the track soil erodes down to the bottom and sharp pointed rocks are left over the surface of the track as the soil erodes, which is a major problem for the vehicles commuting up and down. Such sites require an urgent levelling. Hence, spreading of rock layers one over the other akin to track soling pattern is the need of the hour. After the spreading, tamping with the help of excavator or compaction with the help of a compactor should be complementary. So, for such a task a separate team should be formed, which will do the needful job before or after the actual working hours of the whole project-teams.

Movement of tippers/ earth-moving plants/ mixture machines over the track: Tippers to remain at passing places, preferably towards the hill side, whenever any loaded vehicle is approaching them from the bottom of the hill to the top for supply purposes.

Tips and tricks to save time and manage available resources efficiently

1. Water is the most important entity which is required when we are doing gravity type permanent works. The use of large refined oil tins is really helpful in such a situation. It has an approximately 15 litres of capacity (regular used tins). The advantages it serves are:

a. **Light weight** than the standard equipment (metallic buckets).

b. Let's say we despise metallic buckets and use plastic buckets. Though, the plastic buckets are light weight but they have a very short life when it comes to hard-job usage and especially in such a terrain. So, tins provide **more durability**.

c. **Reduces the administration waste** by employing its utility over the track.

So, the above pros makes it the most desirable resource for water carrying in hills.

2. No doubt employment of mixture machine over the construction sites gives an uncanny advantage over the manual mixture preparation, but at the same it is more important to use that mixture at the same pace. Manually picking up the sand, cement and aggregate mixture creates a time-lag void between the work in progress and the mixture prepared by the mixture machine. So, it is very important to employ a machine which has a bucket attached to it.

In our case, we **used the bucket of 8 tonne excavation machine** (for the drainage line and gravity type permanent works). It provide us a **great work speed** and also **reduced the time-lag void** between the mixture preparation and the work going in progress.

3. Use of ply wood for side walls of the drainage line, rather than manually making the wall with hands also saves a lot of human effort and time. How? Making a hollow template from a pair of plywood in the shape of wall and later on filling it with the sand, cement and aggregate mixture. Tamping of the mixture with the help of a tamping tool is important other wise the wall from the base becomes really weak, due to the presence of uneven mixture at various sites of it.

Cold Weather

Effects of cold weather on walls

Avoid leaving gaps between the wall stones as it may lead to freezing-thawing effect. In this basically the water from the hill occupies the voids in the walls during the day time and at night as the temperature falls to minus degrees, the water in the voids freezes and expands by becoming ice. This expansion further expands the voids and increases its volume. This cycle of freezing and thawing repeats itself on regular basis and hence wall strength reduces over a period of time.

Effects of cold weather on cement concrete*(in the absence of special precautions)*

1. Delayed setting

When the temperature falls below 5° Celsius, the strength of the concrete reduces as compared to the strength of concrete at normal temperatures.

2. Freezing of concrete at early ages

When concrete is exposed to freezing temperature, there is the risk of concrete suffering irreparable losses of strength and other qualities, that is, permeability may increase and the durability may be impaired.

3. Repeated freezing and thawing of concrete

If concrete is exposed to repeated freezing and thawing after final set and during the hardening period, the final qualities of the concrete may also be impaired.

4. Stresses due to temperature differentials

It is a general experience that large temperature differentials within the concrete member may promote cracking and have a harmful effect on the durability. Such differentials are likely to occur in cold weather.

Accelerating Agent

Calcium Chloride may be used as an accelerating admixture in cold weather concrete construction jobs. However, there are certain conditions for the usage of this compound as an accelerator in concrete. These conditions are as follows:

1. It shall not be used in prestressed conditions because of its potential danger in augmenting stress corrosion.

2. Wherever sulphate resisting concrete is required, calcium chloride shall not be used.

3. Avoid using it in RCC works as the threat of steel corrosion is higher due to its usage.

Note:- While making a solution of calcium chloride, add calcium chloride to water and not water to calcium chloride, as it is an exothermic reaction and may cause accidents.

Since most of our work was PCC based and not RCC, so it added as an advantage for us.